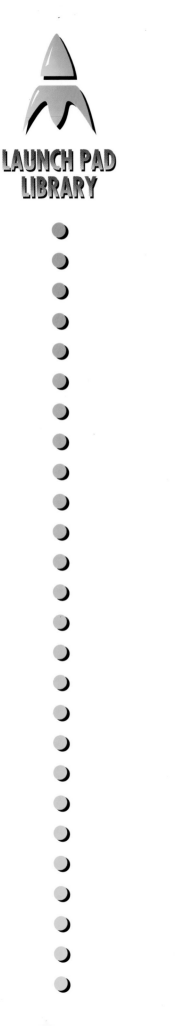

OCEAN WORLD

FRANCESCA BAINES

STAMPLEY

How to use this book

Cross-references
Above some of the chapter titles, you will find a list of other chapters in the book that are related to the topic. Turn to these pages to find out more about each subject.

See for yourself
See-for-yourself bubbles give you the chance to test out some of the ideas in this book. They explain what you will need and what you have to do to see if an idea really works.

Quiz corner
In the quiz corner, you will find a list of questions. The answers to the quiz questions are somewhere in the same chapter. Try to answer all the questions about each subject.

Chatterboxes
Chatterboxes give you interesting facts about other things that are related to the subject.

Glossary
Difficult words are explained in the glossary on page 31. These words are in **bold** type in the book. Look them up in the glossary to find out what they mean.

Index
The index is on page 32. It is a list of important words mentioned in the book, with page numbers next to the entries. If you want to read about a subject, look it up in the index, then turn to the page number given.

Contents

Oceans of the World

Oceans cover over half of Earth. Oceans are huge, but sometimes they are divided into smaller areas called seas. Some parts of oceans are deep, dark and cold, while others are shallow and warm.

The living oceans

Beneath the waves, oceans are full of extraordinary animals, from tiny fish to huge whales. Some of the most important animals are so tiny you cannot see them. They are called **plankton** and are food for larger animals.

Under the water

The bottom of the ocean, the seabed, is not the same all over. It can be muddy, sandy or rocky. Sometimes it is flat, but it can also have mountains or deep narrow ditches called trenches.

▶ It is fun to play in the sea when it is calm.

◀ In some warm, shallow waters, brightly colored coral reefs grow. Many fish search for food or hide from enemies among the coral.

Water on the move
Oceans are always moving. They are pulled by **currents**, which carry water to different parts of the world. Currents are caused by winds, the spinning of Earth and the **temperature** of the land.

Powerful waves
The wind blows the surface of the ocean into waves. On a calm day, the waves are small, but when there is a storm, the waves are bigger and the water becomes rough. When waves crash onto the **seashore**, they slowly wear away rocks on the **beach**.

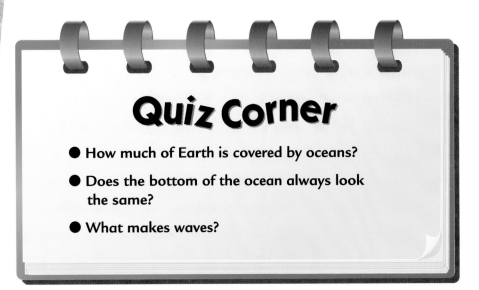

Quiz Corner

● How much of Earth is covered by oceans?

● Does the bottom of the ocean always look the same?

● What makes waves?

5

look at: Oceans of the World, page 4; Shallow Waters, page 10

Seashore

Twice a day, the sea moves up onto the **seashore**, then goes back out again. These movements, called **tides**, are caused by the moon. At high tide, the sea is pulled far up onto the seashore. At low tide, it is pulled away again. Animals that live along the **seashore** are used to living where the water comes and goes.

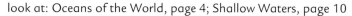

CHATTERBOX

The oceans of the world flow into one another, so things that fall into the ocean may end up thousands of miles from where they were dropped. Often, coconuts are found far away from the tropical islands where they grew.

The anemone catches food with stinging **tentacles.** *If it is attacked, it can pull in its tentacles.*

The scallop belongs to the same group of animals as the clam. Its shell comes in many shapes and sizes.

The lugworm lives in the cool, damp sand. Other creatures, such as crabs, hide in the sand, waiting for the tide to come in.

The water snail attaches itself to a rock with its suckers. Its shell protects it from enemies.

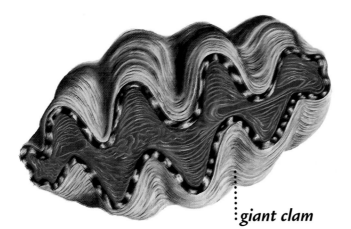
giant clam

Mollusks

The ocean is full of **mollusks** — animals with soft bodies. These animals are an important food for other ocean creatures.

Mollusks live in shells, which protect them. Some mollusks, such as oysters and clams, have two shells, which the animal holds tightly together. When mollusks feed, the shells open. This lets seawater pass over fine hairs that pick out tiny pieces of food. If the mollusk feels in danger, it quickly closes its shell.

oysters

The sea urchin has a soft body protected by prickly spikes. It eats plants and tiny animals on the rocks.

The starfish has five arms, which it uses to crawl over the seabed. If a starfish gets an arm bitten off, it grows a new one.

The limpet is a mollusk with a cone-shaped shell. It grips the rocks so tightly, it is almost impossible to pull it off.

Quiz Corner

- How often does the sea move up and down the seashore?
- Why do mollusks live in shells?
- Where can seashore animals hide when the tide is out?
- What happens when a starfish looses an arm?

look at: Seashore, page 6

The Crab Family

Crabs, lobsters, prawns and shrimp belong to a family of animals called **crustaceans**. They have soft bodies with a hard outer shell called an exoskeleton. This shell protects them from hungry **predators**. Crustaceans eat any food they can find on the seabed and **seashore**.

How crabs grow

The crab cannot grow in the same way as many other animals because it has a hard shell outside its body. When the crab becomes too big for its shell, the shell cracks open to show a new, larger shell inside. This new shell hardens in a few days.

▼ The hermit crab does not have its own hard shell, so it lives in the shell another sea animal has left behind. As the hermit crab grows, it moves to a larger shell.

▲ Crabs have eight legs for walking and two arms with big **pincers** for cutting up and eating food.

Lobsters

Usually lobsters hide during the day and hunt for food at night. One of their pincers is bigger than the other. They use their big pincer to crush **prey** and the smaller one to cut it into bite-size pieces.

◀ The lobster has long feelers, or antennae, that let it know when something is moving in the water nearby.

▲ Every year when storms hit Florida, large groups of spiny lobsters walk in lines over the seabed to calmer waters.

A helpful shrimp

A cleaner shrimp eats tiny animals that crawl over fish. This helps keep the fish clean. Although shrimp is a popular fish food, the helpful cleaner shrimp never gets eaten by the fish it cleans.

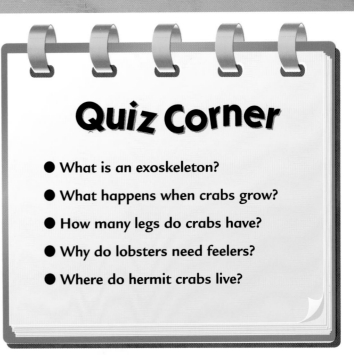

Quiz Corner

- What is an exoskeleton?
- What happens when crabs grow?
- How many legs do crabs have?
- Why do lobsters need feelers?
- Where do hermit crabs live?

look at: Seashore, page 6; Coral Reefs, page 12

Shallow Waters

The most shallow parts of the ocean, where the land slopes gradually into the water, are called **continental shelves**. Here, sunlight reaches almost to the seabed, and plants, such as seaweeds and sea grasses, can grow. These waters are usually warm, clear and full of **plankton**.

▲ Seahorses live among seaweed. When resting, the seahorse holds on to the seaweed with its tail to keep from floating away.

Plants without roots
Seaweeds belong to a group of plants called **algae**, which are different from plants that grow on land. Seaweeds do not have roots or flowers. Instead, they have holdfasts, which attach them to rocks or the seabed and keep them from floating away.

holdfasts..............

▲ Empty egg cases are often washed up on the **seashore**.

A small shark
Dogfish belong to the shark family. They lay their eggs among seaweed in a special case called a mermaid's purse. The purse has strings called tendrils to hold it to the seaweed.

10

▼ Kelps are the biggest seaweeds. Often, many kelp plants grow side by side. They form underwater forests, which sway gently in the ocean water.

Quiz Corner

- What is a mermaid's purse?
- How are seaweeds different from other plants?
- For what does a seahorse use its tail?
- What are the biggest seaweeds called?

look at: Shallow Waters, page 10

Coral Reefs

In a few parts of the world, where the ocean is shallow, clear and warm, there are beautiful underwater gardens called coral reefs. Reefs are made up of many types of coral, such as fans, horns, pipes or plates. Most corals are hard, but some are soft and sway in the ocean **currents**.

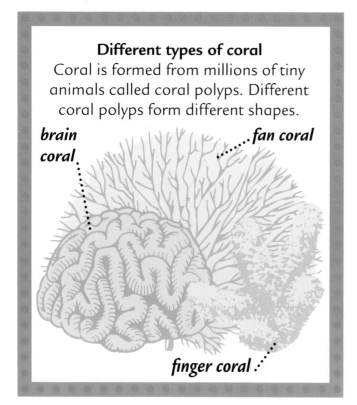

Different types of coral
Coral is formed from millions of tiny animals called coral polyps. Different coral polyps form different shapes.

brain coral

fan coral

finger coral

Hiding places
Coral reefs are full of hiding places, such as tunnels, caves and tiny holes. They make safe homes for many ocean creatures. Some small fish can dodge between the corals to escape from bigger fish that try to eat them.

▲ The Red Sea in Egypt has a large coral reef. Scuba divers find many colorful fish there, such as this saber squirrelfish.

Quiz Corner

- What tiny animals form coral?
- Where do coral reefs grow?
- Why do many sea animals live in coral reefs?
- Where do saber squirrelfish live?

look at: Shallow Waters, page 10

The Open Ocean

The oceans of the world are home to thousands of different kinds of animals. These animals spend most of their time looking for food and trying not to be eaten. Many travel long distances in search of food. Others drift where the ocean **currents** take them.

Life under the waves

Different types of ocean creatures live in different parts of the ocean. Some, such as flatfish, stay close to the seabed to hunt for food. Others, such as turtles, live near the surface of the water because they need to breathe air.

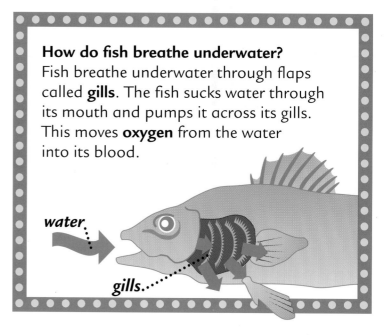

How do fish breathe underwater?
Fish breathe underwater through flaps called **gills**. The fish sucks water through its mouth and pumps it across its gills. This moves **oxygen** from the water into its blood.

water

gills

The sea snake has a flat tail that works in the same way as a paddle. The snake uses it to push itself through the water.

The flounder, like other flatfish, lives on the seabed. It has eyes on top of its head, so it can see what is happening above it.

*The ray has a flat body and fins that look like wings. It seems to fly through the water. The electric ray can give its **prey** a powerful electric shock.*

14

Quiz Corner

- Which parts of their bodies do fish use to breathe?

- Why do some fish travel in schools?

- What does the jellyfish use to catch its prey?

- What does the sea snake use to swim?

◀ A group, or school, of fish swim together for safety.

The flying fish can leap out of the water and skim over the surface.

Shimmering schools

Some fish swim in huge groups called schools. A school can make it difficult for **predators** to pick out one fish to eat. Sometimes a school can even be mistaken for one enormous fish.

The sea turtle lives most of its life in the ocean, traveling enormous distances across the warm waters of the world.

The jellyfish drifts through the ocean, waiting to catch prey in its long, stinging **tentacles.**

look at: The Open Ocean, page 14

Creatures of the Deep

Light cannot reach the bottom of the ocean, so down deep it is always cold and dark. Many deep-sea animals have ways of making their own kind of light to help them see. They are also good at catching food, which is often difficult to find.

Glowing in the dark

Ocean animals that glow in the dark use light in many different ways. Some jellyfish flash to frighten enemies. Anglerfish use light to make their **prey** or a mate come toward them. Others, such as flashlightfish, use light to signal to each other or to help them see when they are hunting.

flashlightfish

◀ The flashlightfish has glowing strips under its eyes, which it turns on and off like car headlights. They help the fish see what is ahead.

▼ This jellyfish glows in the dark and flashes brightly to frighten enemies.

jellyfish ....

◀ The deep-sea anglerfish has a rod that grows from the top of its head. The rod glows to make other fish come toward it. In the dark, prey cannot see that they are swimming straight into the mouth of the anglerfish.

The swallower fish has a stretchy stomach, in which it can hold a fish almost as big as itself. One meal can last the swallower fish a long time.

brittle star

tripod fish .....

..........sea cucumber

.... gulper eel

▲ Brittle stars, tripod fish and sea cucumbers live on the seabed in the deepest parts of the ocean. They eat any food that sinks to the bottom.

▲ The gulper eel swims along with its giant jaws wide open. It eats everything that floats into its mouth.

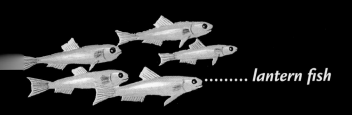

.... lantern fish

▲ Lantern fish are common deep-sea fish. On moonless nights, they rise to the surface of the water to eat plankton.

Quiz Corner

● Why is it always cold and dark deep down in the ocean?

● Why does a gulper eel swim with its jaws open?

● How does an anglerfish catch its prey?

look at: The Crab Family, page 8; The Open Ocean, page 14

Octopuses and Squid

Octopuses and squid belong to the group of animals that have **tentacles**. An octopus has eight tentacles with suckers on the bottom. The tentacles help the octopus move over the seabed. The suckers help it grip its food or anchor itself when a **predator** is trying to attack.

Clever creatures

Many scientists believe that octopuses are intelligent. They have discovered that octopuses learn quickly and can even do tasks, such as taking a cork out of a bottle. In experiments, octopuses have also been known to steal food from one another's tanks.

▼ The squid has eight short tentacles for swimming and two longer ones for catching food.

CHATTERBOX

A giant squid can be over fifty feet long — that's as long as seven divers swimming hand to flipper. There are even stories of these monsters wrestling with sperm whales.

SEE FOR YOURSELF

Octopuses and squid swim by squirting out water from their bodies. You can see this by blowing up a balloon, but not too much, then letting it go underwater. As air escapes, the balloon is pushed off in the same way that an octopus or squid is pushed when it squirts water.

Keeping safe

Octopuses and squid can hide from enemies by changing their color. This is called **camouflage**. They can also squirt out a cloud of dark ink that makes it difficult for enemies to see them in the water.

▼ The giant octopus lives deep down in the ocean. Its eyes are seventeen times larger than human eyes.

Quiz Corner

- How does the octopus move?
- For what does the octopus use its suckers?
- When does the squid use its two longer tentacles?
- When would an octopus or squid squirt out a cloud of ink?

look at: The Open Ocean, page 14; Creatures of the Deep, page 16

Sharks

Sharks are the world's biggest fish. Some sharks are great hunters, with razor-sharp teeth, but others eat only tiny **plankton**. Sharks have excellent hearing and can pick up the sound of splashing water from far away. They also have a good sense of smell and can sniff out animals that are hurt and will be easy **prey**.

A full set of teeth
During a shark's lifetime, it will have had thousands of teeth, which grow in rows. As soon as a tooth from the front row breaks or falls out, one from the row behind moves forward to take its place.

first row..........

second row..........

◀ The sand tiger shark has sharp, strong teeth for killing prey.

The great white shark
One of the most dangerous kinds of sharks is the great white shark. It is a powerful hunter with strong jaws and enormous, jagged teeth. Usually great white sharks eat animals such as seals. Occasionally, they attack people.

Strange heads

The hammerhead shark has one eye and one nostril on each side of its hammer-shaped head. When the shark hunts for food, it swings its head from side to side so that it can see all around its body. Some types of hammerhead sharks are hunted by humans for their skin and oil.

▶ **The hammerhead shark is a fast and powerful swimmer.**

▼ **When hunting prey, the great white shark can swim five times faster than a person. Its smooth, rounded body and strong tail help it to move quickly through the water.**

Quiz Corner

● Why are sharks such good hunters?

● What happens if a shark's tooth falls out?

● Are great white sharks dangerous to people?

● Why are hammerhead sharks hunted?

look at: The Open Ocean, page 14; Octopuses and Squid, page 18

The Whale Family

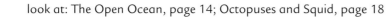

The largest ocean creatures are whales. They are mammals, and need air to breathe. Dolphins and porpoises belong to the whale family. They are called toothed whales and have small, sharp teeth for eating fish and squid. Whales, like all other mammals, need air to breathe. They take in air through blowholes on the tops of their heads.

Big and blue

The blue whale is the biggest whale of all and is probably the largest animal that has ever lived on Earth, including the biggest dinosaur. A fully grown blue whale is about the size of a jumbo jet. This whale is also the noisiest animal in the world. It moans and grunts loudly to other blue whales.

Baleen whales

There are two types of whales: baleen whales and toothed whales. Baleen whales do not have teeth. Instead, they have a row of bristly plates, called baleens, that look like combs. Baleen whales eat only tiny sea animals, such as krill, that can pass between the plates.

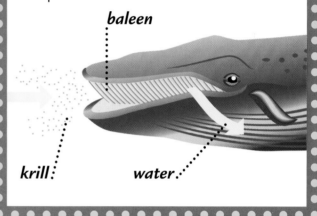

baleen

krill

water

blowhole

Dolphin or porpoise?
Dolphins and porpoises look alike, but there are ways to tell them apart. Dolphins have long, beak-shaped snouts and rounded teeth. Porpoises have rounder snouts and flatter teeth. Dolphins also live in large groups, while porpoises usually live alone.

▶ Bottle-nosed dolphins hunt for fish in groups. They also like to play together and often leap out of the water at the same time.

▲ The blue whale has an enormous appetite. A fully grown adult eats huge amounts of krill every day.

Quiz Corner

● How do whales, dolphins and porpoises breathe?

● What does a baleen whale eat?

● Which has a longer nose, the dolphin or the porpoise?

● Which is the biggest whale of all?

23

look at: Seashore, page 6; The Open Ocean, page 14

Seabirds

Some seabirds live on the **seashore**. They have long legs for wading in shallow water and thin beaks for picking out food from mud or sand. Other seabirds live far out at sea. They are good at flying and spend weeks in the air. When they come back to land, they find it hard to stand up. All seabirds return to the seashore to lay eggs.

◄ Many seabirds spot fish from the sky, then dive after them at great speed.

▼ Gannets, like many other seabirds, live in large groups on steep rocks and cliffs.

SEE FOR YOURSELF

Many gulls lay their eggs on narrow cliff ledges. The eggs do not fall off the cliffs because they are a special pointed shape. If they are knocked, they just roll in a circle. You can test this by making your own pointed eggs out of modelling clay and watching how they roll.

Long-distance flyers

The albatross is a large seabird with long, strong wings. It can fly over the oceans for months at a time. When an albatross flies, it hardly flaps its wings. It simply glides through the air, carried by the wind.

▲ The black-browed albatross visits land only to lay eggs and look after its chicks.

Quiz Corner

● Why do all seabirds return to the seashore?

● How do many seabirds catch fish?

● Which seabird can fly over the ocean for many months at a time?

look at: The Whale Family, page 22

Icy Waters

Around the North and South Poles, parts of the ocean are frozen — but they are still full of life. Animals that live in and around these frozen oceans, such as fish, seals and whales, are used to living in the cold. Seals have thick layers of fat, called blubber, to keep them warm, and some fish have a kind of blood that does not freeze.

CHATTERBOX

No one has ever found a mermaid, but there are many stories about this strange creature that is half fish and half woman. Most people now believe that mermaids are really walruses.

▲ Walruses live together in large groups. They use their two long front teeth, or tusks, to dig for food on the ocean floor. Their whiskers help them decide what is good to eat.

Seals and sea lions

Seals and sea lions look similar to each other, but you can tell them apart. Sea lions walk around on dry land using their strong front flippers, while most seals have weak front flippers and just slide around on their stomachs.

▼ Adélie penguins look clumsy on land, but they are good swimmers. They stay in the sea for weeks at a time.

▲ The seal dives deep down into the water looking for fish to eat. It cannot breathe underwater, so it closes its nose until it comes back to the surface.

Penguins

The penguin is a bird that cannot fly. On land it waddles on its short legs, but underwater it swims as fast as a seal. It uses its wings as flippers to move through the water quickly and its webbed feet to turn. As it swims, the penguin's white stomach makes it difficult for **predators** to spot it from below.

Quiz Corner

● What is blubber?

● For what does a walrus use its tusks?

● Why do penguins have white stomachs?

● How can you tell the difference between a seal and a sea lion?

27

look at: Seashore, page 6

Oceans in Danger

All over the world, people eat animals from the ocean. But nowadays we are catching too many fish and there may not be enough left for the future. Oceans are also becoming **polluted**. We must take care of our oceans to keep them safe for us and the animals that live in them.

Keep it clean

Trash thrown into the ocean or left on the **beach** may lie on the ocean floor or be washed up on another beach. This garbage can harm animals, which may become caught in it or try to eat it. Always take your garbage home and put it in a trash can.

▲ Even large animals, such as this fur seal, can get caught in garbage. An animal may push its head through holes in a net, then find it cannot free itself.

▲ In some countries, factory waste is dumped straight into the sea. This can kill animals living there.

CHATTERBOX

One salmon farmer has a clever way of keeping seals away from his fish. He uses a model of a killer whale to scare them away!

Too many fish?

Fishermen have become so good at catching fish that many countries now have strict rules about how they may catch them. Fishermen are not allowed to use nets with small holes, because these nets catch too many fish. If nets have big holes, young fish can escape and **breed**.

▼ Small fishing boats catch fewer fish than large ships. This means more fish are left in the oceans to breed.

Quiz Corner

- Why do some fishermen use nets with small holes?
- What happens when garbage is thrown into the sea?
- Why should we protect the oceans?
- Can fish nets hurt large animals?

N223H

Amazing Facts

● Dolphins have their own language. They talk to each other by making chirping and clicking sounds.

☆ *Mother penguins can find their own chicks on a crowded iceberg. To the mother's ears, each chick sounds different, and she can pick out her own chick by just listening for its cry.*

● Did you know that whales can sing? Underwater, their songs can be heard for hundreds of miles. The grunting song of the blue whale is louder than the engine of a jet plane!

☆ *The world's smallest fish is the dwarf pygmy goby, which lives in the Pacific Ocean. It is about the size of a baked bean.*

● Male seahorses are good fathers. Their job is to look after the females' eggs. They carry them around in a pouch hidden underneath their bodies until the eggs are ready to hatch.

☆ *The giant blue clam is a type of mollusk that can live for over 100 years. Sometimes it makes a precious stone, called a pearl, in its shell.*

● Sea snakes kill fish with a poisonous bite. Just one drop of their strong venom is enough to kill three people.

☆ *The starfish has a strange way of eating. It can push its whole stomach out of its body and onto its unlucky prey. The prey stays covered by the starfish's stomach until it has been completely digested.*

● Hermit crabs can grow to many different sizes. Some are as big as a human hand, but others are as small as a pea.

☆ *The female sea turtle lays her eggs on a sandy seashore. She leaves the baby turtles to hatch without any help, but they know exactly what to do. As soon as they hatch, they quickly run down the beach to the sea.*

Glossary

algae The family of plants to which seaweeds belong.

beach A stretch of land along the edge of the ocean, usually covered by sand or small pebbles.

breed To make young of one's kind.

camouflage A disguise that hides something, usually so that it looks like its surroundings. This confuses enemies.

continental shelf The shallow part of the seabed just off the **seashore**.

crustacean A creature that has a hard outer shell called an exo-skeleton, instead of bones. Most have two pairs of antennae, two body parts, and gills.

current A large portion of water or air flowing in one direction.

gills A part of a sea animal's body that absorbs **oxygen** from water. Animals with gills can breathe underwater.

mollusks Animals with soft bodies and no backbone. Most mollusks grow hard shells to protect their soft bodies.

oxygen A gas that is found in air and water. Plants and animals need oxygen to live.

pincer A very strong claw made up of two parts that close tightly to hold or cut things.

plankton Tiny plants and animals that live in the sea.

polluted Something that has been damaged by other substances.

predator An animal that hunts other animals for food.

prey An animal that is hunted by another animal for food.

seashore The land along the edge of the ocean. As the tide comes in, water moves onto this land.

temperature How hot or cold something is.

tentacles Long feelers, similar to arms, that can be used to catch or hold things.

tides The rise and fall of the sea level at the ocean's edge.

Index

Published in the USA by C.D. Stampley Enterprises, Inc., Charlotte, NC, USA. Created by Two-Can Publishing Ltd., London. English-language edition © Two-Can Publishing Ltd, 1997

Text: Francesca Baines
Consultant: Mathew Robertson
Watercolor artwork: Alan Male, Stuart Trotter
Computer artwork: D Oliver
Commissioned photography: Steve Gorton

Editorial Director: Jane Wilsher
Art Director: Carole Orbell
Production Director: Lorraine Estelle
Project Manager: Eljay Yildirim
Editors: Belinda Webber, Deborah Kespert
Assistant Editors: Julia Hillyard, Claire Yude
Co-edition Editor: Leila Peerun
Photo Research: Dipika Palmer-Jenkins

ISBN: 0-915741-81-4
Printed in China 2005

Photographic credits: Bruce Coleman (C&S Hood) p12-13, (Hans Reinhard) p25r; Oxford Scientific Films (Fred Bavendem) p18t, (Max Gibbs) p10t, (Howard Hall) p9c, (Richard Hermann) p11, (William Paton) p24-25; Photographers Library p4-5; Planet Earth Pictures (Peter David) p16b, (Ken Lucas) p21c, (William Smithey) p28t, (Norbert Wu) p8b; Tony Stone Images p5t, p20t, p26, p29; Telegraph Colour Library front cover, p23t; Zefa p15t, p19, p27, p28b.